Bibliographic information published by the German National Library:

The German National Library lists this publication in the National Bibliography; detailed bibliographic data are available on the Internet at http://dnb.dnb.de .

Imprint:

Copyright © 2010 GRIN Verlag, Open Publishing GmbH
Print and binding: Books on Demand GmbH, Norderstedt Germany
ISBN: 9783640612635

This book at GRIN:

http://www.grin.com/en/e-book/150103/differences-and-similarities-between-domestic-and-international-hrm

Robert Stolt

Differences and Similarities Between Domestic and International HRM

GRIN Publishing

GRIN - Your knowledge has value

Since its foundation in 1998, GRIN has specialized in publishing academic texts by students, college teachers and other academics as e-book and printed book. The website www.grin.com is an ideal platform for presenting term papers, final papers, scientific essays, dissertations and specialist books.

Visit us on the internet:

http://www.grin.com/

http://www.facebook.com/grincom

http://www.twitter.com/grin_com

Individual Coursework

Managing People in Global Markets

Identify and Explain the Main Differences and Similarities Between Domestic and International HRM

Submission Date: 16/03/2010

Word Count: 2087

Table of Contents

List of Abbreviations

CCT	...	Cross-Cultural Training
CSAs	...	Country-Specific Advantages
EU	...	European Union
HCN	...	Host-Country National
HR	...	Human Resources
HRM	...	Human Resource Management
ICFTU	...	International Confederation of Free Trade Unions
IHRM	...	International Human Resource Management
ILO	...	International Labour Organisation
IR	...	Industrial Relations
M&A	...	Mergers & Acquisitions
MNC	...	Multinational Company
PCN	...	Parent-Country National
TCN	...	Third-Country National
WTO	...	World Trade Organisation

List of Figures and Tables

1 Introduction

Human resource management (HRM) is becoming an increasingly important topic as organisations are forced to adapt their operations to a rapidly growing global environment (Boxall, Purcell & Wright, 2007, pp. 216-218). In this regard, international human resource management (IHRM) has gained in substantiality compared to domestic human resource management in terms of management, organisational structures, cultures and workforce utilisation. The sustainable international human resource management is essential for implementing strategies in multinational companies (MNCs) (Bartlett & Ghoshal, 1989).

Companies generally engage in internationalisation activities for the following reasons: higher profit and sales potential, risk spreading, realisation of competitive or country-specific advantages (CSAs), reaction to competitor actions, capitalisation on government incentives, securing business relations, access to know-how and hedging of currency movements (Rump, 2006, p. 10). From an HR perspective companies need to address issues such as the selection, recruiting, compensation, and legal/regulatory requirements of a 'global workforce' (Du Plessis, Venter, Prabhudev, 2007, p. 59). Overall, the globalisation has led to a heightened acknowledgement of a well-managed workforce (Keating & Thompson, 2004, p. 595). On top of that, this development has also contributed to the view that HRM has become a function of strategic significance rather than simply a support function (Scullion & Starkey, 2000, pp. 1061-1081; Pucik, 1992, pp. 61-81).

The objective of this paper is to provide a clear overview of the differences between domestic and international HRM analysing recent developments and current issues in this subject. The coursework is divided into five chapters. Initially, the general theoretic foundations of human resource management are explained in chapter two. Thereafter, the specific commonalities and differences of domestic and international human resource management will be outlined in chapters three and four, respectively. Finally, in a retrospective analysis of the paper, the research findings will be analysed and an outlook of the future development of HRM on a global level compared to domestic human resource management will be given.

2 Definition of Human Resource Management in a Domestic and International Dimension

Human resource management is commonly defined as a 'strategic and coherent approach to the management of an organization's most valued assets – the people working there who individually and collectively contribute to the achievement of its objectives' (Armstrong, 2006, p. 3). Another definition delineates human resource management as 'designing management systems to ensure that human talent is used effectively and efficiently to accomplish organizational goals' (Mathis & Jackson, 2007, p. 4). Above all, human resource management establishes a foundation for the employment of people, the subsequent development of their capacities and equally using, sustaining and compensating their services in line with the overall organisational provisions. The general human resource activities include human resource planning, staffing, performance management, training and development, compensation and benefits as well as industrial relations (IR) (Dowling, Festing & Engle, 2008, p. 2).

International human resource management encompasses the distinctive features that emerge through the global operations of MNCs in various parts of their processes, summarised in the model below (*Figure 1*).

Figure 1: The Model of IHRM

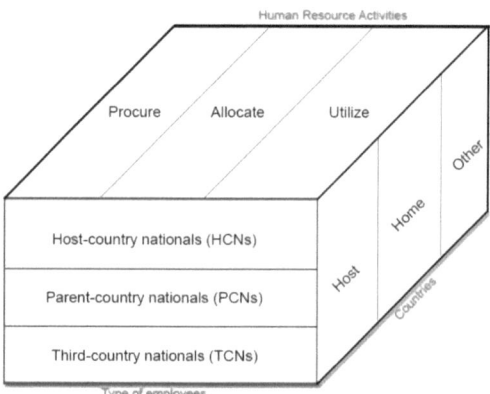

Adapted from: Morgan, P.V. (1986). International Human Resource Management: Fact or Fiction. Personnel Administrator, 31(9), 44.

On the first dimension, these are primarily the characteristics of procurement, allocation and utilisation, while the second category displays the country of operations and the third delineates the three classes of employees of a MNC (i.e. host-country nationals – HCNs, parent-country nationals – PCNs, third-country nationals – TCNs). One common aspect of international human resource management is the emergence of international assignees, commonly known as *expats*. The flow of these expats for multinational companies with international operations is summarised in *Figure 2* below.

Figure 2: International Assignments / Expats

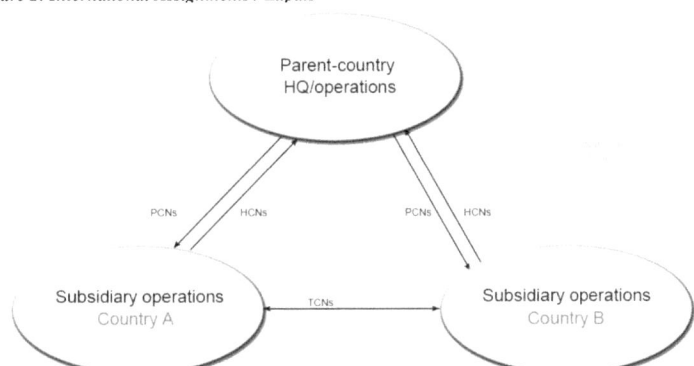

Adapted from: Dowling, P.J., Festing, M., & Engle, A. (2008). International Human Resource Management (5th ed.). United Kingdom: Thomson.

Generally, IHRM policies are far more complex than in the domestic HRM system due to the interaction with different variables (e.g. government and regulatory bodies). In order to gain a broader understanding, the various similarities and differences between domestic and international human resource management will be analysed in the two subsequent chapters.

3 Similarities Between Domestic and International HRM

Comparing domestic and international HRM, a general convergence exists within the basic functions of HRM (i.e. procurement, allocation and utilisation) and there are HRM concepts which are universally applicable. On top of that, these three basic functions of international HRM are generally adaptable to the six main HR activities (human resource planning, staffing, performance management, training and development, compensation and industrial relations). There is also coherence between IHRM and HRM as domestic human resource management is increasingly dealing with a more international workforce, hence the focus is equally placed on topics such as managing the diversity of the workforce (Dowling et al., 2008, p. 3). Moreover, the view of a more geocentric approach to international HRM (which places an emphasis on the abilities and skills of the employees irrespective of their nationality or location) can favour large multinationals' preference for a consistent worldwide HR framework, which may in turn lead to a harmonisation of various domestic HR systems on a global basis (Harzing & Van Ruysseveldt, 2004, p. 61). An important prerequisite for the functioning of the geocentric approach is an interconnected organisation, which facilitates the flow of information and contains system harmonisation strategies as well as the representation of regional and national interests.

In conclusion, one may say that there are certain commonalities shared by IHRM and domestic HRM, however, the methods of dealing with diversity in a singular national frame of reference may not always reflect the plurality of global HR without adjustment. In the following chapter, some of the reasons for the differences between IHRM and domestic HRM will be analysed in more depth.

4 Differences Between Domestic and International HRM

The differences between domestic and international HRM are generally attributed to the inherent level of complexity and uncertainty of operations in other countries, rather than variations in the HRM activities (Dowling et al., 2008, p. 5). In addition to this, there are other variables that influence the differences between domestic and international HRM, such as the industry in which the multinational is positioned, the cultural environment, the reliance of the multinational on its domestic market and the attitudes of senior management (Dowling et al., 2008, p. 9) (*Figure 3, p. 5*).

The additional complexity of international HRM activities can result from the heightened number and heterogeneity of decision-making factors as well as the inherent liability of foreignness, which leads to more complex cause-effect relations. Furthermore, environmental constituents are not always stable and differ in various countries, thus require the multinational to engage in situation-specific, case-by-case actions. Addition-

ally, the linguistic plurality affects communication and cooperation patterns and preju-
dices can exist among different nations (Reisch, 1997, pp. 10-15; Düfler, 1991, pp. 191-
192; Scherm, 1999, 127-128). According to Dowling et al. (2008, p. 5) the complexity
of international human resource management depends on the following factors: the extent of business activities, a more global perspective, consideration of employees' personal sphere, greater risk potential, the mixture of the workforce and the significance of
broader legal, economic and socio-cultural factors.

Figure 3: Variables Moderating Differences Between Domestic and International HRM

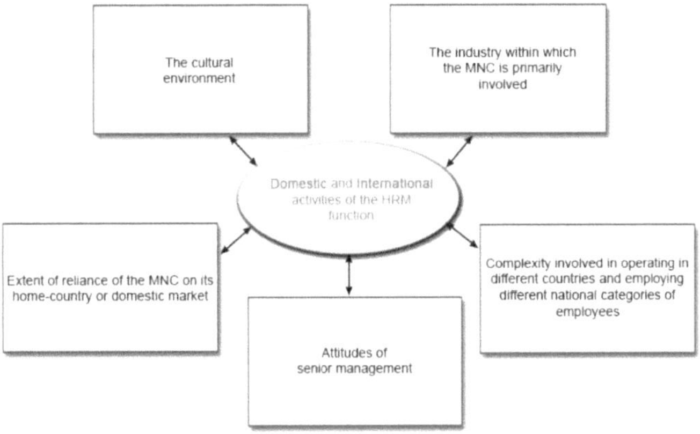

source Management. Management International Review (MIR). 3/99, 31.

Regarding the extent of business activities the human resource department needs to ful-
fil a number of functions which would not be found in their domestic markets. These
can range from international taxation and relocation, host-government relations over to
translation services and administrative services for expatriates.

Secondly, a broader more global view of issues is necessary for a globalised company
with regard to the variables of human resources and complexities of activities (e.g. a
globally consistent pay/reward system). According to Gross and Wingerup (1999, pp.
25-34), this interconnectedness will eventually lead to a standardised global remunera-
tion system based on the skills and competencies required in the global workforce. In
contrast to that, complex equity issues exist when foreign nationals are given preferen-
tial treatment in terms of compensation. The current methods to determine international

pay rates by linking the base salary to local market rates, such as the 'Going Rate' and the 'Balance Sheet Approach', may solve some of these issues but still comprise certain disadvantages, such as disparities between expatriates of different nationalities or potential re-entry problems (Dowling & Welch, 2006).

Thirdly, complexity is added through more involvement in employees' personal lives as a significantly higher amount of support is needed (e.g. accommodation arrangements, schooling for children or recreational programmes).

The risk exposure is another important issue as MNCs face particularly high direct costs and potential indirect costs such as loss of market share and reputational damage (Dowling et al., 2008, p. 8). Examples for foreign market-entry risks are expatriate failure (Scullion & Collings, 2006, pp. 59-63) and political (e.g. military conflicts or civil and social upheavals) or terrorist violence (Harzing & Van Ruysseveldt, 2004, p. 79).

Another essential consideration is the variation in significance as the mix of expatriates and locals varies (i.e. the increased employment of locals leads to an emphasis on activities such as local staff selection, cross-cultural training [CCT] and management development) (Dowling et al., 2008, p. 7).

Lastly, there are additional external influences (i.e. economic, political and social), which constrain a globally uniform approach to HRM. These can for instance be government-driven factors (e.g. programmes to enhance employment and training opportunities for own nationals), local regulations (e.g. health and safety, taxation, labour regulations) and local business practices (e.g. gift giving).

In addition to complexity, there are four other influence factors on the relation between IHRM and domestic HRM.

The first moderator is the cultural environment, which describes a distinct way of life, set of attitudes, values and behaviours which members of a community adopt over time (Briscoe & Schuler, 2004, pp. 113-135). IHRM needs to appreciate the predominant differences in the cultural environments in which an organisation operates together with the organisation's own culture. Major research in this field has been undertaken by Hofstede in his book *Culture's Consequences: International Differences in Work-Related Values*. Considerable differences in parent and host country cultures can also lead to conflicts (e.g. nepotism) or culture shock. *Figure 4* (Appendix, p. 12) summarises the phases usually experienced by expats moving abroad.

Moreover, the degree of reliance of the multinational on its domestic market is another essential consideration. In addition to the size of a firm, the size of its domestic market may have considerable implications on the 'multi-nationality' of its operations. *Figure 5* (Appendix, p.) indicates that multinationals based in countries with extensive domestic markets and a large population, thus high consumer demand (e.g. USA), are inward-looking (i.e. Slow internationalisers or occasional internationalisers in case of a small firm), whereas small countries such as Switzerland, Netherlands or Sweden are outward-looking as they rely largely on foreign markets to extend their customer base (i.e. enthusiastic internationalisers). As a consequence, HR practices need to reflect these conditions and should be structured accordingly.

Another moderator of the differences between IHRM and domestic HRM is the industry type. Two distinguishable forms of industries exist: *multidomestic* and *global industries*. The former being characterised by essentially independent national competition (HRM is domestically oriented, e.g. retailing), the latter features multinational and interlinked competitive structures (HRM should be locally responsive while at the same time ensure global consistency, e.g. aircraft industry) (Briscoe & Schuler, 2004, pp. 38-49).

Lastly, the attitudes of the senior management towards international operations are an essential criterion for determining whether a company will operate internationally or not. The typical reasons behind the failure to establish a global mindset (and thus the development of a globally-oriented staff) are inward-orientedness, lack of information, ethnocentrism or cultural insensitivity.

5   Conclusion and Outlook

In a retrospective analysis of this paper, one may say that MNCs need to think globally taking all the complexities of activities and HR functions into account. Notwithstanding the fact that there is some convergence in HRM concepts around the globe, there are certain differences between domestic and international HRM. International HRM undertakes all the important activities such as human resource planning, staffing, performance management, training and development, industrial relations and compensation in more depth and is thus inherently more complex.

Looking into the future development of international human resource management one can say that there are forces of change (such as global competition, mergers and acquisitions [M&A], advances in technology and communications) that require MNCs to be flexible, locally responsive and committed to knowledge sharing and competence transfer (Bratton & Gold, 2001, pp. 73-77). Especially large corporations will benefit from a worldwide HR system. A general theme that will continue in the future is the convergence and divergence debate of international HRM resulting from globalisation. Some experts argue that continued divergence in national patterns of economic activity and employment relations has led to the notion of 'varieties of capitalism' while others say that pressures towards convergence (e.g. in the EU or Asia) may lead to commonalities in cultural and institutional contexts.

While IHRM has an expansive outlook and requires awareness of individual institutions (e.g. the World Trade Organisation [WTO], the International Labour Organisation [ILO] or the International Confederation of Free Trade Unions [ICFTU]) and influence factors (e.g. national legislation and economy, local practices and cultures), HRM only has to recognise and deal with *one* organisation's culture and the domestic legislation. In summary, it can be said that the complexity caused by the different economies, cultures and national institutional profiles has a large role to play in the differentiation of domestic and international HRM.

Reference List

Armstrong, M. (2006). *A Handbook of Human Resource Management Practice* (10th ed.). United States: Kogan Page.

Bartlett, C., & Ghoshal, S. (1989). *Managing across borders: The transnational solution*. United States: Harvard Business School Press.

Boxall, P., Purcell, J., & Wright, J. (2007). The Oxford Handbook of Human Resource Management. United Kingdom: Oxford University Press.

Bratton, J., & Gold, J. (2001). Human Resource Management: Theory & Practice (2nd ed.). United States: Lawrence Erlbaum.

Briscoe, D.R., & Schuler, R.S. (2004). *International Human Resource Management*. United States: Routledge.

Dowling, P.J. (1999). Completing the Puzzle: Issues in the Development of the Field of International Human Resource Management. *Management International Review (MIR)*, 3/99, 31.

Dowling, P.J., Festing, M., & Engle, A. (2008). *International Human Resource Management* (5th ed.). United Kingdom: Thomson.

Dowling, P.J., & Welch, D.E. (2006). *International Human Resource Management* (4th ed.). Australia: South-Western, Thomson.

Düfler, E. (1997). *Internationales Management in unterschiedlichen Kulturbereichen*. Germany: Oldenburg.

Du Plessis, A.J., Venter, F., & Prabhudev, N. (2007). IHRM and HRM: Two Sides of the Same Coin? The *International Journal of Knowledge, Culture and Change Management, 7*(4), 59-69.

Gross, S.E., & Wingerup, P.L. (1999). Global Pay? Not Yet! *Compensation & Benefits Review, 31*(4), 25-34.

Harzing, A.-W., & Van Ruysseveldt, J. (*2004*). *International Human Resource Management*. United Kingdom: Sage Publications.

Keating, M., & Thompson, K. (2004). International human resource management: overcoming disciplinary sectarianism. *Employee Relations, 26*(6), 595-612.

Lysgaard, S. (1955). Adjustment in a foreign society: Norwegian Fulbright grantees visiting the United States. *International Social Science Bulletin*, 7, 45-51.

Mathis, R., & Jackson, J.H. (2007). *Human Resource Management*. United States: South-Western College Publication.

Morgan, P.V. (1986). International Human Resource Management: Fact or Fiction. *Personnel Administrator, 31*(9), 44.

Peng, M.W. (2009). Global Strategic Management. United States: South-Western.

Pucik, V. (1992). Globalization and human resource management, in Barnett, C.K. (ed.), *Globalizing Management: Creating and Leading the Competitive Organization*. United States: Wiley.

Reisch, B. (1991). *Euromanager – Internationale Personalentwicklung an der Schwelle zum europäischen Binnenmarkt*. Insitut für interkulturelles Management. Germany: Bad Honnef.

Rump, J. (2006). *Internationales Personalmanagement*. Germany: Fachhochschule Ludwigshafen am Rhein.

Scherm, E. (1997). *Internationales Personalmanagement*. Germany: Oldenburg.

Scullion, H., & Collings, D.G. (2006). *Global Staffing*. United States: Routledge.

Scullion, H., & Starkey, K. (2000). In search of the changing role of the corporate human resource function in the international firm. *International Journal of Human Resource Management, 11*(6), 1061-81.

List of Appendixes

Appendix

Figure 4: The U-Curve of Cultural Adjustment

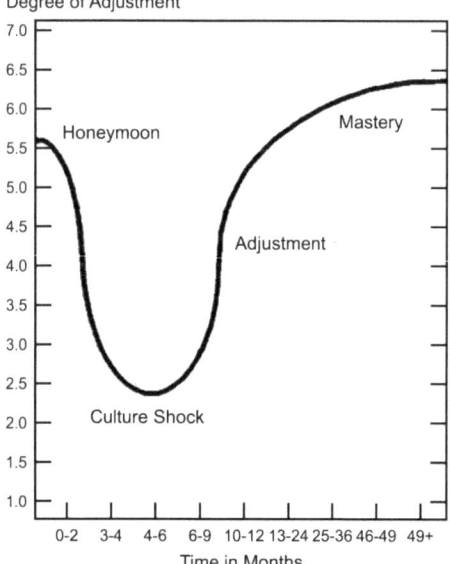

Degree of Adjustment

Adapted from: Lysgaard, S. (1955). Adjustment in a foreign society: Norwegian Fulbright grantees visiting the United States. International Social Science Bulletin, 7, 45-51.

Figure 5: The Propensity to Internationalize (Market size/Firm size Matrix)

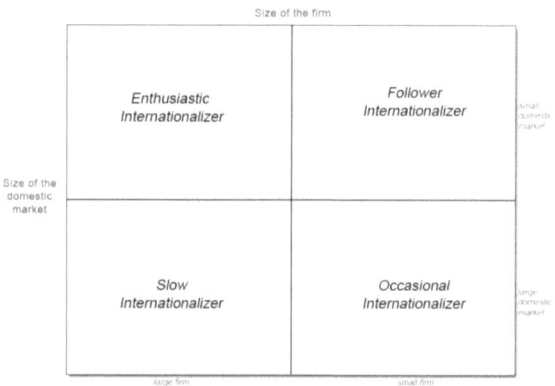

Adapted from: Peng, M.W. (2009). Global Strategic Management. United States: South-Western, p. 158.